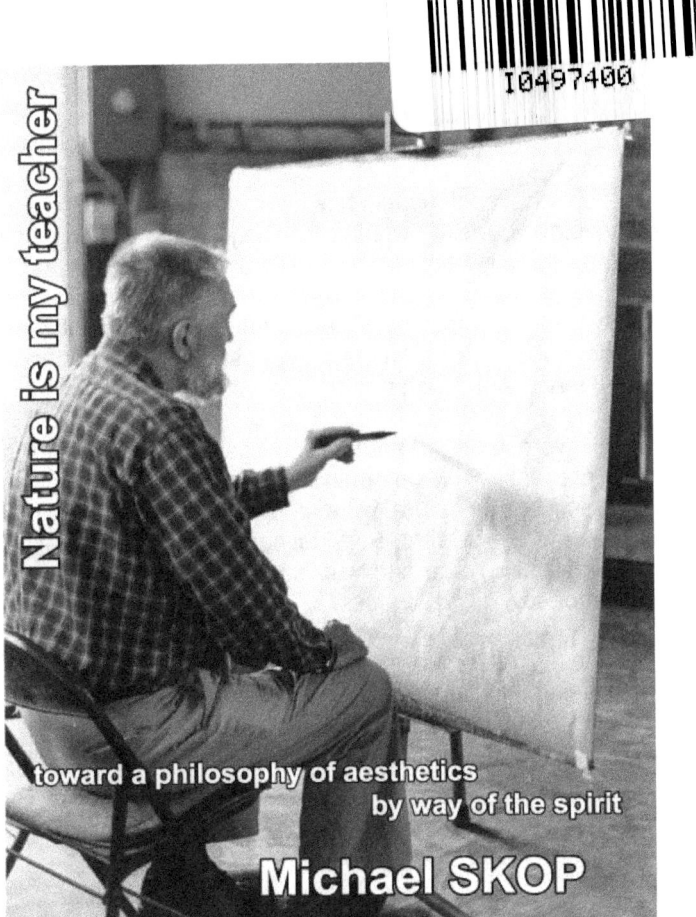

**Summary**

"I have trained myself to let nothing pass by."–Picasso.

I hope that each aspect has given you enough insight to develop your skills within art. The journey is a long way and nature is very complex in its dynamics.

The above quote by Picasso should be part of your vocabulary or manifesto in establishing concrete evidence along with nature.

The word "train" is an important aspect that requires a lot of practice and determination. You cannot go further, investigating, nature without developing certain skills that are set within the guidelines of this book. It is a wonderful voyage and very stimulating in its dynamics personally.

What is presented in this book is only the beginning awaking into nature and your personal perception.

**Introduction**

"It's a long way there, and.... Yet, it is right next to you."

What do you mean by that professor?

"You will spend the rest of your life learning about nature and about yourself."

The quote is from my professor, Ivan Mestrovic. I didn't realize that importance of that statement until I reached the age of 27. I was dwelling upon aesthetics, putting things together, so that I could make sense of what I had learned in my formative years at Syracuse University. Years of experience in developing concepts has given way to producing this book for your examination. It is important to realize the uniqueness of each facet, so that you can form your opinion(s) about the twentieth and twenty-first century art. There are elements in the book that require some discussions with your colleagues to get a closer picture of the book's objectives.

You can't take it lightly in examining the book since each aspect depends on the next to have a meaning. It is clear for the person who wants to have a unique understanding with nature. One must realize that great artists had a profound experience philosophy. Their greatness has given us insights in this book that will help you substantiate their philosophical thoughts.

I want to wish you a fulfillment and success in life. I hope that this book opens the door or adventures for you to develop your skills.

-Michael Roe Skop

**Glossary**

In some cases, the definition is in the realm of aesthetics and requires the instructor to develop parallel concepts for the student to understand the care of the word.

Plastic: material
Plastic: in reference to a false presentation
Plastic: to manipulate; to take out of; to extract
Plasticity: to manipulate; to take out of; to extract; and to revert back to
Designare: in Latin- This is the entomological not for fun drawing and for design. The principle is the same for both classes.
To Draw: to make a matrix; to extract (to extract and to make a mark requires potential as the part and parcel in a given image.
Parcel: many parts comprising a total of given entity
Static: to repeat in beat; to remain the same (as absolute, as an overtone, to a given entity)
Dynamic: A functional entity reflecting into numerous entities, having energy
Form: Tony and Pete, form is described in multi-facets and requires a lengthy discussion.
Form: Mike's objective is seen from the spirit as a central energy to a given composition.
Design: Design is the sum of a total; Reflecting into a sum changing its meaning to a total)
"The author is George Santayana" 1892-94
Composition: "Com' means all together, "pos" to place in an existence, "ition" refers to total
Order: The relationship of entities in a functional given form
Structure: The relationship of an entity to another in a sustained/machtached state
Balance: There are two ways of interpreting balance. One, is in the realm of a privation.

Privation: Everything belonging to one. All components that are the makeup of a given entity.

Form: I have spent fifty years in this area of concentration. I am still learning. I align my thoughts to Zen concept's congenital philosophy)

Spirit: Found in the realm of being. It is central to the making of a character, a personality and life itself.

Nature: The process or functioning of a given entity or being.

Environmental: a location or place in which things exist

Outline: I was taught not to consider an outline as a given means to creating an image. It is very detrimental to creativity. An outline is an absolute and would mislead a student from the reaching source of the spirit.

Academic:    Aca- to take
             Dem- a rule
             ic- the possession of it

92% of the artists are in academic principle. There needs to be static rules to achieve a goal. Where we are today is in the realm if time, space and spirit. It takes a student four years to achieve those goals.

Absolute: A given perimeter having distinguishing factors leading to conclusion

Non-absolute: Is conceived in the realm of time and space and spirit leading to infinity.

Immediate: Confronting a given object having absolute configurations. The answer us external for the individual, relies in the static forms/objects as an answer to his composition.

Infinity: (must be seen in the realm of aesthetics) A given piece is viewed as timeless in concepts It has a beginning and an end.

Beginning: Having a given power to a given composition.

End: A continuation without any conclusions.

The above information needs some elaboration to clarify the numerous objectives. There is a wonderful feeling that has come over me, and it is viewed as senility. It's wonderful to forget things in life.

<u>Aesthetics</u>- "aes" means essence.
    "thetis" means having the face of
    "ics" possessions of it
<u>Methodology</u>- "Meta" essence
    "hodus" a way of and across
    "ology" the branch of knowledge or wisdom
<u>Form</u>: is perceived holistically
<u>Overt</u>- that which is observable.
<u>Convert</u>- that which is hidden.
<u>Anoptic</u>- worm's eye view; beginning from the bottom perceived celestially.
<u>Catoptic</u>- birds eye view; looking downward; having mundane forms.

These definitions help the student overcome any obstacles that might arise from holistic thinking.

The Analytical/mechanical layout, listed below, is a prime example of the academic approach that is being used today. The objective, with this layout, was to create of present a degree of depth in the reduction of objects in each setting. Figures and buildings were laced in the space as a stage for happenings. The layout became a permanent method as a part of their composition. Schools, universities, and art academics employ this method as means of establishing space.

- Systems and formats are major entities to their composition.
- The renaissance artist did not realize they were creating absolutes within the framework of their composition.

- This approach was detrimental to the laws of nature and man.
- Man is the center and vanishing points for all things come from nature.
- Man, now perceives distance as vast in dynamics.
- He now realizes he is the center for all things that happen in nature.
- Man, also realizes that form and nature exist in the present and offers us generosity and excitement of her dynamics.
- The conceptual world produces a tremendous amount of <u>need</u> as a vital source to the composition.
- The spirit becomes the main issue and the driving force and all things.
- Imagination leads to infinity.
- One can gather by the layouts that the vanishing point reverses itself, helps the artist to achieve greater expectations than ever before.

**Social Static World**
This is a very, very sensitive segment of aesthetics and philosophy. Those who teach in this area need to be well versed in defining the meanings and the parameters of each word and turn. It is essential to begin talking about these issues during the first week of a program of course. The instructor will find it difficult in developing curriculum that will help the student reach the maximum in his creativity and fulfillment.

The social static world has developed static concepts that are used in communicating ideas and information. We need this source of information is a means of developing criterions and daily deeds. In the field of aesthetics, one must use words and terms that are viable to the creative process or processes. I will now give you words that are detrimental to creativity. See, at the left half of the page words that are in the absolute and tangible.

- Proportion: is a form of measurement and reaches conclusions.
- Figure: is a category which explains certain characteristics.
- Front, side, or back: denotes areas or location of a given piece.
- Different colors: denotes an absolute; reuse this source of information daily and therefore static.
- Size: describing tangible items which leads to an absolute and therefore static.
- Divide: using only the rational faculties in establishing proportion.
- Materials: using media as a vehicle
- Beauty: leading to a standard is an absolute.
- Beauty: in descriptive leads to an absolute.

There is an endless of array of words that you can refer to that is used daily that has static qualities. I just gave you a few examples of the words that are used daily at universities, academies, and art schools.

I began my schooling in aesthetics at a very early age. I didn't realize how words and terms could be devastating to a person who wants to understand life and nature. The formative years of my education made me realize that I associate with should be patient to anyone who has selected fine arts as their vocation.

1. Being: we have always viewed our sculptures and drawing in the realm of being.
2. Spirit: Viewing being automatically takes you into the functioning of a figure or a head.
3. Intangible: Van Gogh refers to this term in his writing to his brother Theo. We perceive today that everything is in the dynamics of time and space.
4. Plastic: continuously expressed in the studio.
5. Plasticity: also used on a daily basis.
6. Form: Form for us grows out of the spirit.
7. Scale: considering the extreme parameter of a given thing, used on a daily basis.
8. Monumental: seeing things in an intangible world.
9. Symbolism: is perceived in the intangible and non-absolute world.

"A genius believes more than he thinks."-Rodin

**Spirit is the Vehicle**
The rational mind has always been perceived as an answer to the development of our skills. We look to programs that offer us formulas and systems that are pertinent to our goals. Course outlines that we find in colleges are filled with rational ideas. I was always taught, from the age of nineteen, that the spirit is the vehicle and stimulus to the rational world. It is only through the spirit that one can attach fulfillment.

You will notice by the diagram below that the spirit is much larger than that of the rational mind. Because of this spirit we can attain and develop our skills to the fullest.

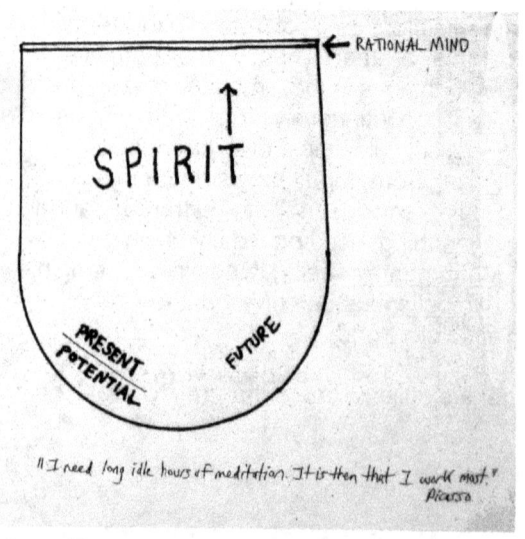

"I need long idle hours of meditation. It is then that I work most."-Picasso

Western culture has always taught us to use our rational faculties to develop our disciplines. They didn't realize that the terms and words would lead us to the dynamics of <u>telling</u>. We verbalize our emotions thinking that it is answer to our spiritual needs. The one who has a composition in the realm of showing is giving himself from the spirit. The great art of today comes from the spirit. I believe that we will always strive for perfection because of the spirit. In Man's quest in the future, no matter what vocation it is, the spirit will dominate his intellectual beliefs.

There are very few instructors who teach this approach and I hope that man will endure to pursuit that which is eternal.

# WESTERN MAN

> THE IMPORTANCE OF THE RATIONAL MIND IS THE ULTIMATE
>
> SPIRIT

Beginner: Usually in narrative
Approaches form in Silhouette
Composition is in Silhouette

1. Student depends on advice.
2. Looks at techniques as the answer.
3. Mind is on "How" do I do it.
4. Craft oriented.
5. Requires established rules.
6. Leads to conclusion.
7. Composition is in techniques.
8. Composition is in rite wrong.
9. Project is key to his conceiver.

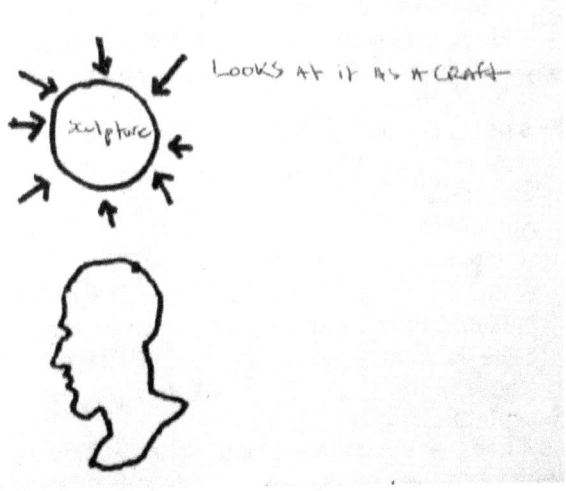

1. Narrative: students in this category are looking at a sculpture piece in static (to repeat in beat) Dynamics.

2. Student requires information that will enable him to portray <u>like images</u>.

    1. Depends on "how" Dynamics and formulas.
    2. Measurement is the key issue for likeness.
    3. The absolute in object is measured in shape/object.
    4. Technique is heavily considered as an answer to the composition. (Beauty is not considered as part of composition.) Aesthetics has no value to this person.

"Right wrong" are the main principles.
Person strives for satisfaction.
The media is the answer for his objective.
Studio/plate is his working space.

Around the sixth week of school students begging to show some confidence. He or she is boarding their concepts into the falling areas of connotation.

The student is working in immediate dynamics:
- Sees action, immediate.
- Sees details.
- Student concerned with right and wrong.
- Composition leads to the Absolute.
- Achieves the dynamics in a four collective Maurer.
- Intuition/instinct is governed by their subjectiveness.
- Style is introduced in super financial dynamics. (clichés)

You'll find these students caught up in developing self-esteem and their egos. Also, the students tend to be bull-headed as they seem to know the answer. Their answers, for the most part, are in the realm of the absolute. Their images lend to absolute/tangible conclusions.

These students must be handled carefully as they may react to a negative/critical comment.

Categories, collectively, leads this individual to a tail conclusion.
1. These students look at categories having titles. Therefore, the approach to the composition is the realm of telling.
2. Images, and its shape, tend to be their style.
3. Style grows originally out of ego.

Dynamics in is negative (word for word)
Reasoning in (telling)
Object is man issue (Model)

1. Details key issue to likeness
2. Sculpture appears segmented.
3. Measurement past of composition
4. Right and wrong
5. "How do I do it?"
6. "Where should I start?"
7. "What is the purpose of doing it?"
8. Preference for media
9. Front, side, and back are key issues.
10. Degrees

Action is part of composition.

Reasoning is in the immediate

The model in the answer

The artist works with the idea of "I like it"

The artist is in telling.

The artist is deceptive.

The artist is very conscious of ego.

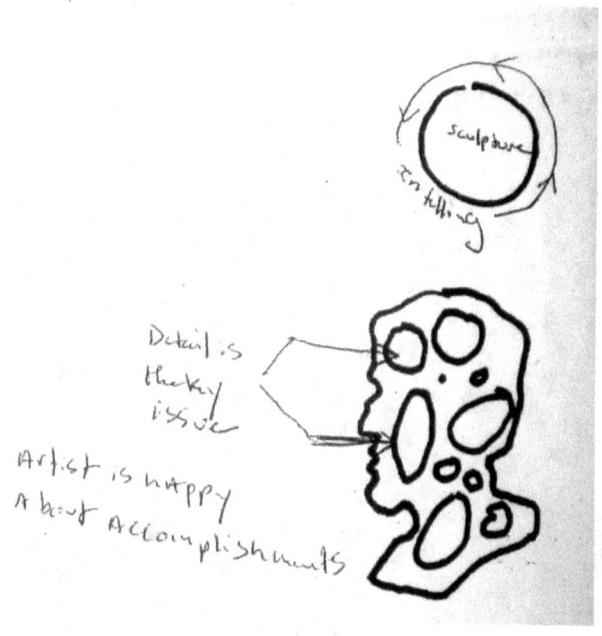

**Literal (word for a word)**

1. Texture dictates the composition.
2. Profile leads to categories and eventually to thieves.
3. Title starts the composition and brings it to a conclusion in titles.
4. Action is in physical terms and expressions are in immediate shapes.

This person likes what he does and looks at things as evidence.

5. Satisfaction requires praise and affection.
6. Studio/place is where creativity develops.

This student does not have inspiration of a desire that leads to a conviction.

7. All knowledge leads to circumstance. It is the circumstance that is part of composition.
8. He/she looks at the professor in scheduled time.
9. This person us highly frustrated and requires the instructors insight/s.

Dynamics in Idealism
Establish rules and methods.
Confidence is in detail.

1. Telling the root of the composition
2. Bad and good are the key issue to composition.
3. Works mainly for the collector.
4. No evidence of spiritual harmony
5. The artist is not conscious of the spiritual nature.
6. The artist perceives detail as the answer.

7. Likeness can composition is in comparative analysis.
8. Texture is part and parcel to this person's composition.
9. Ability to achieve pm principles of right and wrong.
10. Requires a system to motivate person growth.
11. Looks at composition in a finished state.

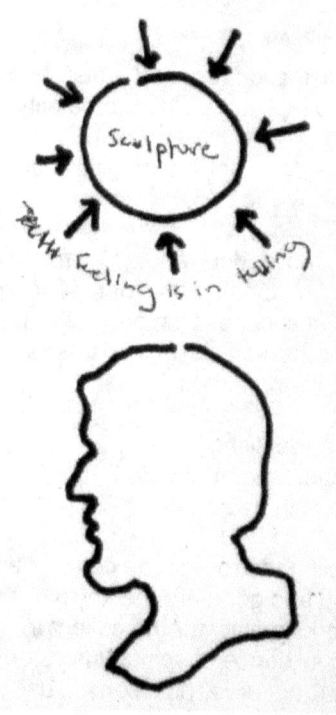

**Idealism: Personnel and Cultural**

Tradition is the key issue.

- Composition: Personal Preference to 60%
- Composition: Cultural 40%
- Composition is linear.
- Composition has physical linear movement.
- Texture is a key issue.
- Form begins to show human dynamics.
- Stages is part and parcel to the composition.
- Psychic Dynamics is part and parcel to the composition.
- Psychic Dynamics is part and parcel to composition (1890)
- Drama
- System is personnel and cultural.
- Measurement
- Expression is in the realm of telling.
- The artist demands excellence from her/him seld
- Unity of form is growing.

"You must see the whole part" - Michelangelo.

Revelation from the 19th century

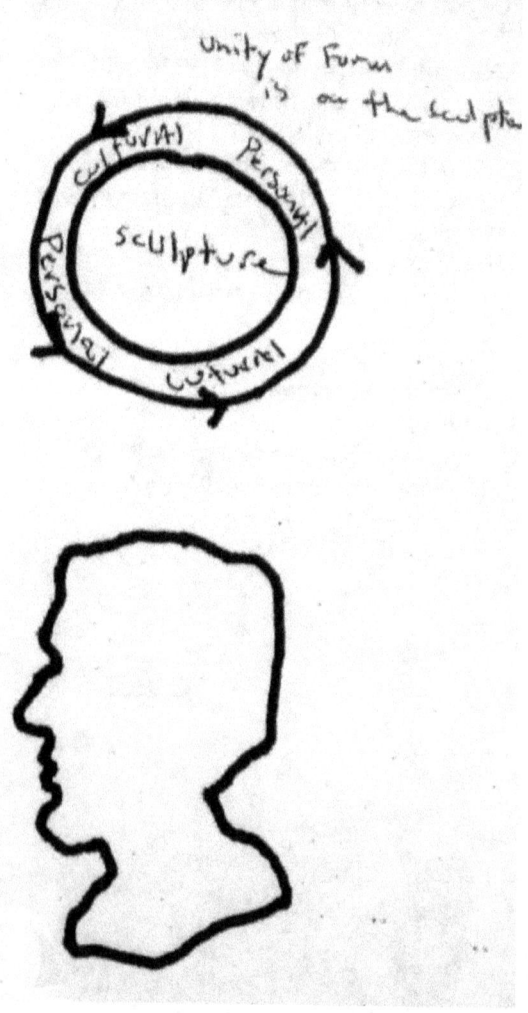

## Idealism

Ideal: To place in an observable state.

Examples: Art, done in this category, can be found in Russian Nationalism and Neoclassical Movement in France during the period of 1800-1840.

Higher education, with western men, have always presented courses in this category. There is a tragedy that evolves from this discipline; it destroys creativity. There is always a premise that establishes concepts in absolute principles.

Here are the following to expect from their point of view:

1. Rules, the Golden Rule of the early 1800's is a prime example for establishing composition.

2. Systems and formats are guidelines for establishing excellence in the composition.

3. The composition must look interesting and requires the artist to fulfill the themes in the painting.

4. What is "wrong" is established and what is "right" is also established.

5. The artist must serve the cultural principles and objectives.

6. Measurement, standard, physical structure, a little of plastic

7. Man being concerned with categories, titles, differences, preferences, selections lead the artists to rational "telling" in their composition. Where

images, are the mainstream of thinking, the artist will eventually produce additive type absolutes in their results.

I am very concerned about these concepts, as it requires years and years of training. There is an endless array of systems that are embedded within the framework of our society. It is in this area of concentration that you and Pete need to visit me in Kentucky. I look at this area as a Pandora's Box filled with bad systems. It destroys creativity, inspiration, and aspiration. It is in this area that individuals will disagree with me.

I have spent my life, of 71 years of dwelling about narrative, concepts, literal concepts, ideal dynamics, and universal principles. I can assure you, what I'm giving you will require constant experience of examining who you are and your relationship with nature.

8. Personal and cultural principles can be found in the artwork of Rodin. There is 30% cultural dynamics between 40 and 45% personal dynamics, and 25% from the spirit.

9. The artist is very concerned with being satisfied with his/her composition and looks at oneself as an individual. He/she is constantly going with the idea of making it right and fixing his/her composition better.

10. This artist is very dogmatic and is very much interested in making his/her composition better.

11. You will find that this artist, seems to be, concerned with principles that exist in "how to do it" dynamics.

I cannot, present this information in its entirety, as it is endless and boggling in its scope.

I have always been taught to perceive myself as a universal being and not as in individual.

Mediocre minds are always found among individuals.

<u>Geniuses are always universal in principles.</u>

<u>All great art is universal</u>.

**Idealism**
1795-1840

Approach is the Golden Rule (Systems and methods)

1. Approaches in the realm of right and wrong.
2. See's thing as projects
3. Technique's part and parcel of composition
4. Physical movement part of composition
5. Realm: elegance, nobility, grace are mandatory for composition.
6. The absolute in measurement is also part of composition.
7. Structure is seen as physical.
8. Deeds are socially oriented.
9. The artist works for what is noble.
10. System
11. Drama

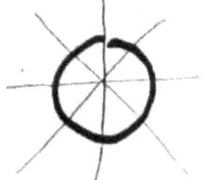

Rep. tion of A particular System

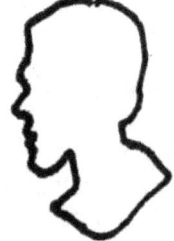

## 20th century thinking
Universal
Dynamics: is in the time and space

1. Composition is now within man.
2. Composition is now in unity form.
3. Composition is in the spirit.
4. The artist is married with nature.
5. The "intangible" is very to the composition,
6. Time and space is where plasticity exists.
7. Structure is spatially plastic.
8. Harmony grows originally from the artists' spirit.
9. The artist now perceives from conceptually.
10. "Nature has no skin nor core. She is both, one inside and out."

Picasso: "You must reduce the head to an egg."

- Artist perceives in the dynamics of being,
- The artist sees him/herself with nature.
- One must avoid doubt or questioning (this is within the realm of the universal.)
- The spirit must prevail as the source for the composition.
- See yourself as the center Cézanne. "*The outline of the form escapes me.*"
- Sculpture is a catalyst reflecting one's personal energy.
- Beingness leads to personal needs.
- Spiritual and beingness leads to truth.

Approaches form in silhouette

- Student depends on advice.
- Looks at techniques as the answer.
- Mind id on "How" do I do it.
- Craft oriented requires established rules.
- Leads to conclusion.
- Composition is in techniques.
- Composition is in right and wrong.

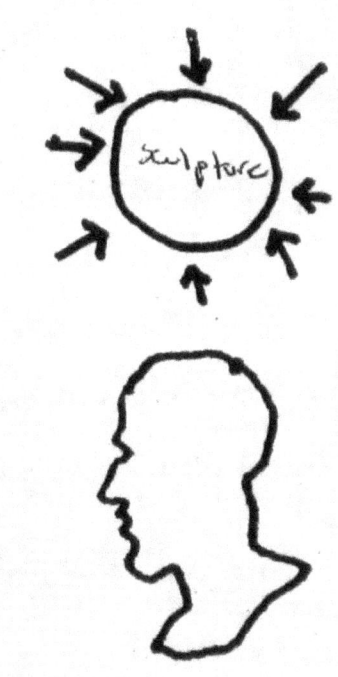

**Universal**

Of or pertaining to the dynamics of nature.

1. Beauty is in the realm of plasticity.
2. Time and space make plasticity.
3. All forms in time and space do not have boundaries nor absolutes.
4. All forms exist in the dynamics of new.
5. Concentration is the key and answer to fulfillment.

6. The artist, now, finds nature as his studio.
7. All life in is the dynamics of time.
8. The artist is highly inspired him/herself in the realm of discovery/need.
9. Fulfillment now exists in the realm of the intangible.
10. Freedoms in the realm of the intangible (not within grasp).

Tangible – within grasp.

The balloon, training aid, is an excellent example for helping students to understand the <u>power</u> of composition. They need to practice the use of this balloon for at least two months. All guest artists have had power to their composition. The power grows organically out of the spirit.

"The outline of the form escapes me." –Cézanne.

**Universal**

1. The intangible is where the power is
2. The intangible is where is clarity is.
3. The intangible is where the wholeness is.
4. The intangible makes the tangible elastic (Matisse)
5. The intangible is where the style grows organically out of the spirit.
6. Symbolism is in the intangible for this person.

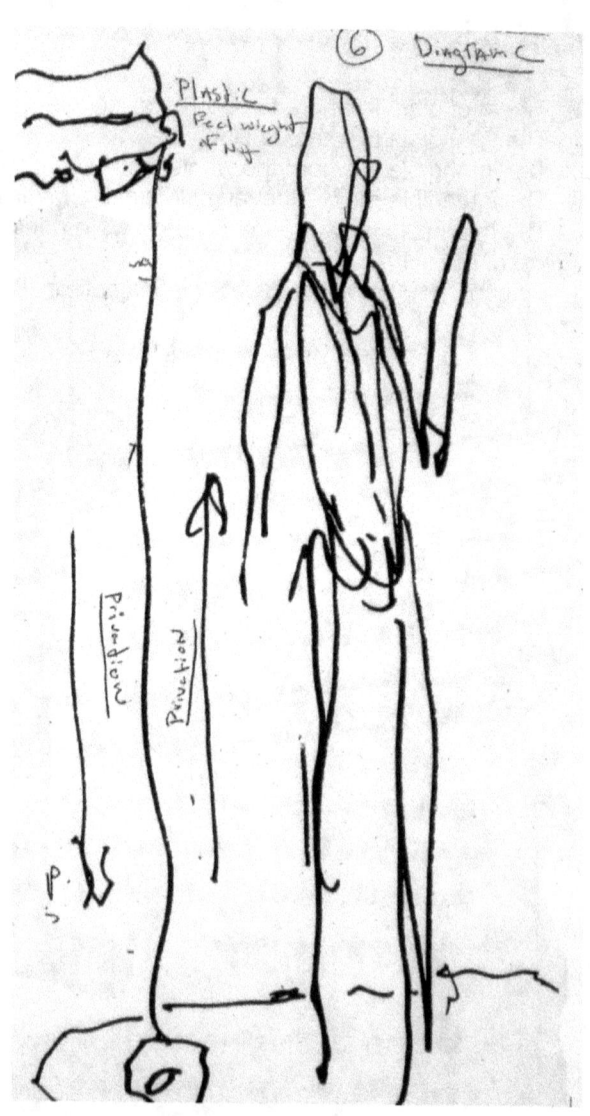

1. This training aid helps to active plasticity.
2. Plastic (to manipulate, to take out of.)
3. Plasticity (to manipulate such as to wake out of and recruit back to.)
4. "Dourbe ve repicefre alle tutto nello un poste" – Michelangelo You must see the whole on the pout.
5. "And the pout must be seen in the whole." – Michael Skop. What I added brings the above principle to the 20$^{th}$ and 21$^{st}$ century thinking.
6. These principles lead the composition to a tremendous amount of freedom and fulfillment.
7. It is always growing to future schemes. Self-esteem grows organically out of the spirit.
8. The artist sees him/herself as universal.
9. The artist is not convinced with style and themes.
10. The artist finds himself constantly struggling with nature.

There is so much to say in this category, universal dynamics, that I find myself being tasked by the idea of it. There is no way in hell that I could write it down in absolute terms. Making diagrams and sketches and verbal communication is the only way to get the idea across to you.

I purposely left out idealism since it requires me to spend considerable time in explaining as parts of both historically and Twentieth century concepts. I know what I have in me begun at the age of 18 these dynamics are very precious and rewarding for me. I have seen many artists lost in the maze of academic principles. I find sadness for them, and I know that life must go on now. I have taken four years and have put it into a few words for you. There are very few of us that teach these dynamics. I hope I didn't confuse you with the information I gave in those categories. It is very easy to open a Pandora's Box and look for explanations. Each aspect that I have given you requires weeks and weeks of work and insight. I look at this in formation religiously. Time and teaching have honed these ideas to a precise state.

The road ahead for a universal thinker is very, very hard. It requires a lot of courage from you.

"You must cherish the talents you have and never underestimate them." -Mestrovic

"When you are in the universal you must have a lot of courage as learning is a daily experience." –Mestrovic.

A Zen Master, which I am, learns every day of his life.

My two assistants still teach me, and I have an open mind for it. For fifty-three years I have kept an open mind and I thank God for the talent that he gave me.

"Ego", is one thing that the young artist must deal with. A result stemming from such a personality causes clinches and superficial structures in their artwork. Now, I would quote Noguchi, "I am not an individual. I am universal in nature." Noguchi.

Now here are the following guidelines:
1. You must perceive yourself continuously in the realm of nature 24 hours/ 7 days a week.
2. Nature is your studio.
3. Preparation is the most vital part within the realm of inspiration. (See quotes)
4. Insight into nature leads a student into fulfillment.
5. Time/space is where form takes on reality. Man now sees himself as the center of all things.
6. It is crucial for young artists to understand that every day is a learning experience. He/she will spend their entire life evaluating himself/herself to nature.
7. We see the world in two components, tangible and intangible. (Obtain definition from dictionary)

## 20th and 21st century/aesthetics
## Universe Principles

The universal idealism is found within the realm of belief. Man, now, is viewing himself as a conceptual thinker. He realizes that everything comes to him and, therefore, he is the center of the composition. This area of concentration is so vast in scope that one is required to participate in discussions. Terminologies, ideas, and concepts, vary among individuals and again require etymological definitions.

Rodin's quote aptly will give you concrete evidence as to universal principles.

"A genius <u>believes</u> more than he thinks." – Rodin.

I have found this quote as pertinent to investigating nature and myself. I have, religiously, pursued all my investigations over a period of fifty-two years. I have found that "belief" makes the composition powerful and plastic at the same time.

One cannot, in this area of concentration, see himself as an individual. It is very detrimental to his fulfillment and the struggle one has with nature. I have found this to be true and have accepted it as my constitution.

The intangible world is far greater than the tangible. Realizing this aspect would lead the artist to a tremendous amount of power and inspiration. We, therefore, see time in the present and, along with space, as leading us in the direction of the spirit and infinity.

The universal aspects are very sensitive in nature. It requires you to prepare yourself for the dynamics of nature.

The conceptual and perceptual values are the primary concern/ or concerns with the artist. All great art has universal principles and reaches us through the language of nature.

The artist in this area of concentration always struggles in his quest for composition. Like, a flower, struggles to be alive in their composition.

Proverb from the Bible- "Forget the past, the things of long ago remember not. See, I am doing something new."

Van Gogh used this proverb as part and parcel to this investigation of nature. Nature is always new, and it requires to see it in the perspective.

I have used this biblical proverb as part of my guidelines in obtaining the numerous meanings found in nature and in man.

Artists like Noguchi, Miro, Picasso, Henry Moore, Rothko, and Baziotes have universal principles in their works of art. These artists have laid the foundation to future investigation/investigations within oneself and in nature.

I have found Zen has parallel structures found in universal principles. A Zen Master, who learns every day, in tuned-into universal dynamics.

I, in my teaching, have used certain training aids so that a student would understand the perspective of universal concepts. Individuals who, see themselves as universal, will readily see themselves as associating with nature as a teacher.

I conclude by saying that the above is only the beginning. I am 71 years old, and I have taken my first step to the reality of universal nuances. The spirit is where you will grow from my teaching. I have given such information to my daughter Ahna, so that she sees herself as a universal being.

**Symbolism**
Sym- of many
Bolic- to churn
Ism- perpetual

This area of concentration requires hours and hours and hours of investigation. Symbolism exists in two distinct realms of investigation: aoptic and catoptic. Catoptic values are mundane (pertaining to earth qualities in nature.) Anoptic pertains to celestial qualities found in relation to man in nature.

I have spent years, and a lifetime, studying the signs and symbols in relation to man and nature, students, those that have studied with me, have spent years and years dwelling on the subject.

An excellent book on this subject is the *Pedagogical Sketch Book* by Paul Klee.

Sym- of many
Bolic- to churn
Ism- perpetual

Sign: is in the realm of the absolute and tangible

**Narrative**

82% to 86% of the artists are in the domain of this realm. You will find students organizing their thoughts in the dynamics of differences. Each entity has a given title. The student feels safe when he/she is directed to tangible comprehending evidence. The following list below is part and parcel to their thinking evidence. The following list below is part and parcel thinking process:

1. Symbolism is at the conclusion of their experience.
2. Right and wrong gives them a degree of direction in their composition.
3. These students tend to get burred with a certain given display in front of them.
4. The student, young artist, needs immense amount of guidance.
5. These artists rely on academic principles.
6. The tangible is within the realm of the sign and dictates, at the conclusion, to symbolism or symbolisms.

This area of concentration requires training aid principles as a means of reaching objectives.

**Symbolism**
Literal: word for a word

1. The symbolism begins to dominate to a slight degree. It influences the sign/tangible giving way to a sense of freedom.
2. Action/movement is precisely the main objectives in these dynamics of symbolism.
3. Beauty, therefore, is to achieve dynamics in rational/telling formulas.
4. There is great number of absolutes in the composition which affects the total composition. One may call these absolutes as being static in nature. Experience(s) "signs" are very evident in the make up in the direction of the composition.

I have found myself in concentration from the age of 19 to the age of 25. It was without a question a tremendous struggle to reach the universal principles found by Picasso, Henry Moore, Noguchi, Rothko and Baziotes. I remember when I was in Germany, I came across a sculpture by Kurt Schwitters. Viewing his sculpture made me think of what I needed to do in my work. With hard work and a lot of practice I achieved the universal principles found by modern masters.

**Symbolism**
Personal Idealism

About 10% of the artists are in this category. They are concerned with established past principles as a means of reaching objectives. They feel very confident to portray something that reaches a certain degree of satisfaction. They require a lot of praise and wish to follow trends in society. One needs to have lengthy discussions about creativity, about ego, and character.

The above information is in addition to the prior aesthetic principles sent to you last week.

I have spent a few years in this area of concentration and realized the parameters that confined me in my work. I took a proverb from the *Bible* that led me down the path to universal principles. "Forget the past. Remember not. See I am doing something new." Van Gogh took this same quote as part and parcel to his composition. He realized, as I did, that nature is always in a new <u>state</u>. Composition, therefore, is in the realm of infinity that grew from the concept of newness.

*You have a long road to walk, and your first step is nature.*

**Symbolism**
Personal/Cultural Idealism

The neoclassic period of 1800-1840 had established guidelines for the young artist to pursuit in their composition. There was a wrong way and a right way to do things and the artist had to succumb to their beliefs. These aspects still permeate colleges and universities and art institutions. The guidelines, without question, destroy the basic premises system, and have eventually stifled me to a great degree.

Formulas set by society influenced the personal growth of artists. There is a tendency to control certain methods that would lead to a satisfaction in their composition.

**Symbolism**
Universal Idealism

Symbolism, in this area of investigation, is in the realm of preparation and the future. We are looking at an area of research and discovering nature's function and man's relationship to it. I am, soon to be 71 years old and I'm still learning about symbolism. A Zen Master spends his daily routine examining himself with nature and the spiritual world. We see, now, that symbolism creates a great degree of power, fulfillment, and spiritual inspirational energy. The twentieth century revelation has given man the opportunity to further his wisdom through universal principles.

I would love to quote the following from Einstein. "The greater investigation that one achieves from nature enhances his wisdom to go forward."

All great art, whether it is Miro or Noguchi or Rembrandt, is universal symbols in their composition. Great artists have always an intense philosophy that grew out of nature. The artist, sees himself as the center and the conceptual world is slowly becoming the main vehicle in developing ideas and concepts in art.

What I have given you with this philosophy is the beginning of a wonderful end with life.

**Explaining Two Premises**
I would like the two presentations to be submitted at this point in time. The first, has to do with the history of <u>quest</u> within the realm of art/aesthesis/philosophy. The second aspect has to do with holistic thinking. These two areas of thought are very critical to forming concepts that are vital to $20^{th}$ and $21^{st}$ century composition. There is a beauty, in man's quest, that one must continuously nurture throughout one's life. We need this source of information as it helps to establish insights and revelations with nature.

Let us define the word quest: To reach excellence; through a procedure of analytical thinking and principles.

In quest there is always a set of goals that has developed from predicaments and obstacles.

It is, therefore, interesting to a young artist who wants his/her vocation to be in the fine arts. These information's helps to establish a nature outlook on and toward life itself. One cannot look at this information as something trivial or not having bearing on a personal philosophical thought. The young artist needs to decide about his/her vocation early on in life. It is a long road to fulfillment, and a long road to achieving a spirit that is central to growth.

Know the value, and the preciousness, and the concept helps in developing one's personal style.

The style grows organically out of the spirit and has an enormous amount of power within the composition. One does not need to be serious about these principles as everything in nature is natural and only requires the young artist to be dedicated and honest with himself/herself.

I am presenting this with the idea of a planning to elaborate on the subject soon. I, also, want you to know that I look at this information as very religious in nature.

Nature to me is a bible and I place all my faith in nature and God at the same time.

So, therefore, the history of a quest and holistic thinking it is very precious to me.

## Holistic Thinking

In 1945, a group of philosophers gathered at a convention to discuss the issues of holistic thinking. Their purpose was to establish perimeters and give the full meaning within the dynamics of their objectives. They wanted to be sure that a young artist of philosopher would be able to correctly translate the full meaning of this term(s).

Holistic thinking: All and encompassing such as all the senses and the entire mental process or processes within man's being.

At the age of 19, I was introduced to the concepts of Secessionism. The philosophy that I and attached from

Ivan Mestrovic's allowed me to venture into other areas of concentration.

Phenomenology, Zen, and holistic thinking became part and parcel to the makeup and directions that I have taken for the last 50 some years. It was a struggle for all this time as I realized that nature has in store for me. There are times when I feel very alone with myself knowing that my teaching involved a tremendous responsibility to my students.

Since holistic thinking is very intricate, it may cause confusion and needs a verbal presentation requiring a tape recorder. I have asked my two assistants to be here for at least a couple of lectures so you may substantiate their views with those views I have just disclosed.

Teaching this information is extremely hard and could easily zap one's energy with beginning students. I remember Christ saying to Peter, "You shall build my church upon this rock." I just have given you a rock, and in nowhere in hell can someone argue points about its deficiency. One must have an open mind in taking this information.

I need to reiterate some of the information I presented to you in my last letter. I need to emphasize the importance of holistic dynamics as important to the artist of this century. It is without question a new dynamic, since 1945, that is awakened the great artists of today. I need to look at this area of concentration, religiously. I, personally, have been involved in it for a period of fifty years. One could spend a lifetime examining all the intricacies of nature. I would like to present the following quotes which substantiate the pursuit of holistic thinking: "I need long idle hours of meditation; it is then that I work most." –Picasso

"I look at the model and go away for six days coming back to draw the model." –Henry Moore

"A line must breathe. If it doesn't, it is a corpse."-Miro

"A color must grow." –Miro

The above should be taken seriously, not as information, but as an insight and revolution. <u>The above quotes will help you mature as an artist.</u>

I have found from my teaching experience that artists venturing into these dynamics have found themselves extremely frustrated. I, too, went though it at an early age, 19, and had decided that my life should be spent learning every day of my life. My two assistants have decided that this dynamic opens a great vista of thinking and does not in any way infringe on one's personal creativity.

When one realizes he or she is the center of all things then the conceptual part of man becomes the vehicle to a spiritual reality.

The five senses are the way we start teaching students. We present this, at an early age, so that the student realizes that all balances, structure, plasticity, and fulfillment make up composition. We no longer look at art as a visual experience since it has a limitation in parameters. Visual artists have the tendency to collect ideas and images that comprise their composition. Visual artists can only reach satisfaction in their work. A wholistic thinker finds him/herself struggling to achieve goals. He/she sees him/herself married to nature and 24 hours/7 days a week in a year.

With that mind the artist is always inspired and realizes that it develops a need within one's shell.

Picasso, Miro, Noguchi, Henry Moore, Baziotes and Rothko are good examples of holistic thinking. They have proven to all of us how to perpetrate the psychological spirit within man. Today the composition grows organically out of the spirit. It nurtures our feelings and spirit that is central to a human being.

A holistic thinker is very much like the tulip bulb that is tuned with nature in a pure way. Beauty for a holistic thinking sits within the realm of our conceptual world.

You may select this area of concentration, or you can deny it. It you venture in this area of thinking it will require a tremendous amount of responsibility. I wish you well.

The need always produces a struggle within oneself. Satisfaction is not part and parcel to this person's thinking. He realizes that the vanishing is within his conceptual world. He no longer looks at the vanishing point as reaching the horizon line. Talent, for a holistic artist, is within the five senses and experience. He demands that being/spirit is central to his composition. The artists who look at visual experience can only reach satisfaction.

I had to reiterate this information to you, as it will be your first step toward nature. We cannot measure our accomplishment as we are learning everyday of our lives.

I'd like to quote Mestrovic: "*You must plant yourself among strong flowers, as it will affect your character and personality."*

I have produced many strong flowers and that is my reward for teaching students.

"It is a long way there, but it is right next to me."

In my previous presentation I did not elaborate enough, in content, about the approach to certain aspects of sculpture. I am taking this opportunity to add the necessary information so that a clarity can give you a better perspective in sculpture.

I have spent most of my life thinking about nature and the process of its function. I am always learning, each day, about nature and myself.

I'd love to quote Picasso when he said "I need long idle hours of meditation. It is then that I work the most." I look at flowers, trees, and the boat in the current and I let my mind drift like the boat in the current. Sooner or later, it gets precise."

My life has been based on this principle and I have found it to be of great use to me. You need to realize that great artist looks at nature as their studio. The four diagrams I presented to you here will help you understand what it takes to achieve those goals.

I have told my students the following: "One cannot go home or leave home." I have found personally that no one can go home or leave home. The primary home is nature. That is your home. You cannot leave it. You cannot go.

You must realize this concept truly changes your wide life and gives you a tremendous amount of clarity and inspiration. It, also, helps you in becoming a mature artist. What I presented to you is the answer for searching nature to its fullest. Those who work in the "how" dynamics are shaped oriented. Those who work in the fourth diagram, realize that nature is the answer.

I have always said to my students to learn about different cultures. It is important as it expands your knowledge and inspiration for your own work. There is an excellent book for someone who is persuading fire arts.

I have pointed out, earlier, that I think holistically. I want to present the following: Walking is part and parcel to the make-up of holistic thinking.

I am thinking of the Zen gardens and its internal and external designs. You can learn a lot from Zen and I do want to point out the importance of African art to your vocation.

African art is not primitive in concept. It is very sophisticated and is closely related to Nature.

**Diagram 1:** we have the example of a person approaching the sculpture in shape dynamics. He or she considers shape as an answer for establishing likeness. The approach is in the immediate and does not have any content/form. He or she feels extremely competent and looks to him/herself as achieving images in parallel concepts. You will find this approach is prevalent among beginning students.

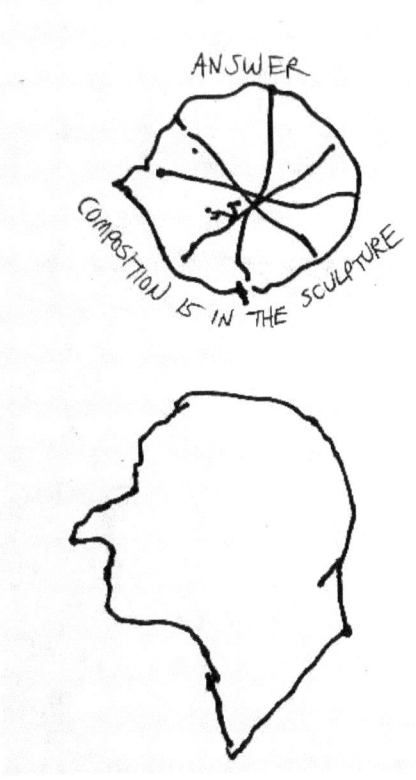

**Diagram 2:** After considerable time, the artist begins to look at details as an answer to achieving likeness. Each area is very important to the individual and builds self confidence in this manner of approach.

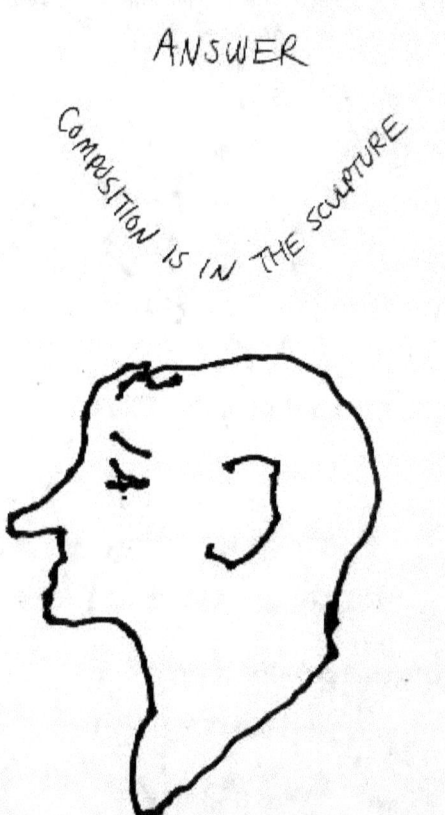

**Diagram 3**: This area of concentration takes considerable time for the person to learn about this craft. He or she needs to know that the use of one piece of clay grows into the next and the next until it reaches fulfillment. That process is where likeness exists. Rodin and Mestrovic taught us this approach and I have used it all my life.

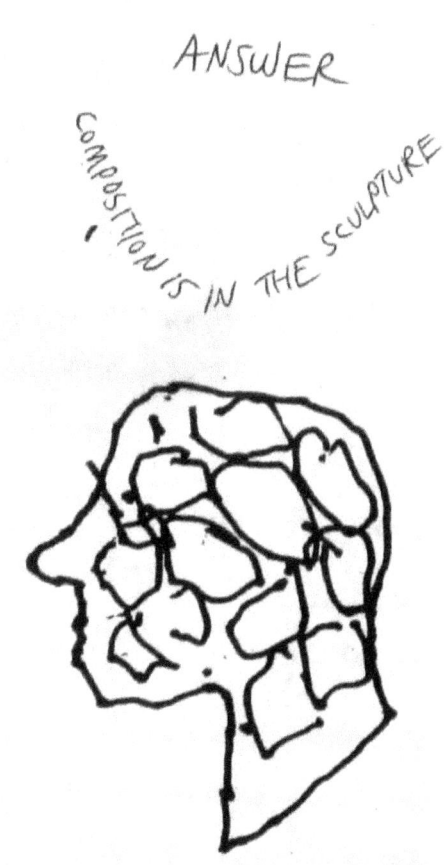

ANSWER

COMPOSITION IS IN THE SCULPTURE

**Diagram 4**: The composition is in man. We now realize that the unity of form can only have its power when it is controlled by the conceptual/perceptual world. This process takes a long time for a person to grasp in its fullest degree. I would like to quote Henry Moore to the following: "It is a struggle in the process of achieving this goal."

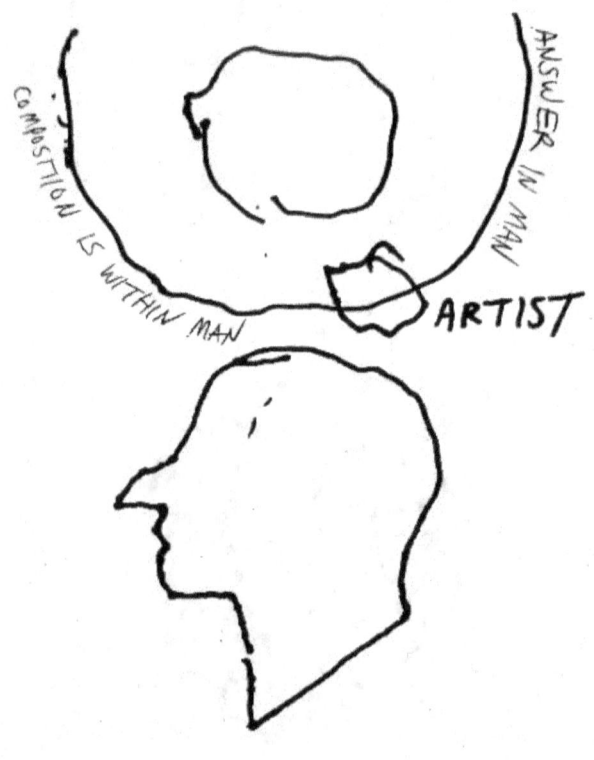

## Chapter 2

There are two excellent books that should be part and parcel to your aesthetics vocabulary: Jacque Maritain's book "Creative Intuition in Art and Poetry: and the book by William Barrett titled "*Irrational Man*". Both books convey to a certain degree, the basic elements in the diagram 5 presented to you. Page 205 in *Irrational Man*, you will see a character devoted to the philosopher Heidegger. You need to read it carefully and look at the diagram as a source for your insight. There is enough information there to help you achieve the most sensitive aspects of aesthetics. I remember my graduate students discussing certain issues that Heidegger had presented in that chapter. I, myself, have always looked at Heidegger as a great source for inspiration. Once must keep in mind that "love: opens many channels of thinking giving way to answers and inspiration.

I would like to quote Matisse at this point and time because of the diagram I presented to you:

"The outside world is transparent." -Matisse

"The conceptual perception makes it possible to stabilize the world of the immediate." -Matisse

"I need long idle hours of meditation. It is then that I work most." –Picasso

The Picasso quote proves that imagination is the key and answer to your imagination. Nature us constantly bombarding us with information pertaining to its functions and its existence in a plastic state.

To understand the diagram completely one needs to put into practice what has been presented. Get a glass (transparent) bowl as a means of exercising the concept presented. Take a piece of paper to exercise what is required of you.

If you could imagine, while sitting there, the world around you. You will notice that the sky meets the horizon line and gives you the impression of sitting in an upside-down bowl. You will notice immediately that the world of imagination is enormous in its existence: It's beyond the world of the senses. Imagination takes over and stabilizes the world of the senses. The diagram shows that imagination gives a lot of freedom to the immediate world of the senses.

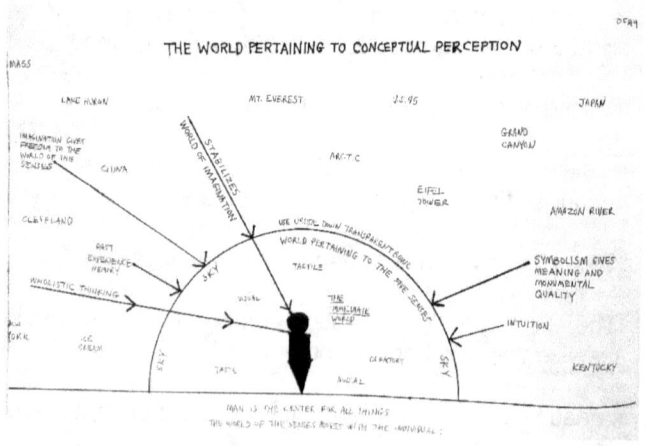

This presentation is the hallmark to all the information that was previously sent to you. You are looking at 53 years of research, developing concepts and ideas that has led to the dynamics of beauty and beautiful. This is an area that needs considerable time to explain all the different facets that is perceived I find it redundant to talk about issues of western culture. My objective, with you, is to go into an area of beauty that is the ultimate in dynamics. There are three quotes that I would like to present to you as pertinent to the 21st century thinking about beauty.

The first two quotes are from Miro's philosophy and should eventually be part and parcel to your vocabulary:

"Color must grow." –Miro

"Line must breathe, if it does not it is a corpse" –Miro

Let us take the first quote and examine it carefully. What does growing mean? It means that it contains time and space and present. So, we realize why this quote that beauty exists within the realm of time. We, also, realize what beauty is always in a free state.

Let us consider the second quote of Miro. The word breathe also implies time and space and freedom. This quote is showing us that the human factors beauty is in the realm of time and space.

The third quote I have considered is very precious to me. It is a quote from the proverbs in the Bible and should be considered as part of your vocabulary.

"Forget the past, the things long ago, remember not. See I am doing something new."

We have here a powerful statement that Van Gogh used as his person philosophy. It gave him a tremendous insight about nature and faith. This quote is making us realize that the rational mind is not the answer for our composition. This quote is reminding us that believe is the substructure to our concept of beauty and that which is beautiful. Let us consider the aspect of what is new as the subjective and objective of our research. Here, again, we realize that new is where beauty exists continuously. New implies a tremendous so beautiful: It is always pursuing what is in its existence.

I think the following two presentations are very critical to understanding the plasticity of beauty. <u>Any form that has great content of the spirit is always plastic in nature</u>.

Let us begin with the two diagrams shown on the next page. You need to memorize this aspect as it will help you immediately in your world.

I have always looked upon my life as a free man. When I was young, I realized, from my professor, Mestrovic, that the spirit is and should be central to my objectives as an artist. I looked at nature intensely and found myself relating to the spirit of the lion. When I examined the lion carefully, I realize that he was tamed by the forces of nature. He was highly sensitive and used his senses to the fullest degree. I said to myself that I too want to be tamed by nature. I realized that nature frees me continuously even to today I have looked upon myself as a lion among my peers. I have found many answers to what beauty is and beautiful and monument in character. Mike is the voice of the lion and of nature. Everything that I presented to you growls inside of me.

Of disciplines as working in the realm of being, life and spirit. Projects only lead you to absolutes and in maternalism. You must be careful when you are working with a given piece. Always remember that nature is your studio, and your thinking needs to be tuned in to your conceptual world.

We realize that front, side and back are locations, and therefore, should not be part of our vocabulary. When you are doing a portrait of someone you must look at is as you perceive an egg. You will always be tuned into life, being and the spirit. A quote from Picasso, "You must reduce the head to an egg." It should be obvious to you that above given aspects needs a lot of practice and training. You will surely grow into a mature artist. Don't allow life to slip by as it is very, very short.

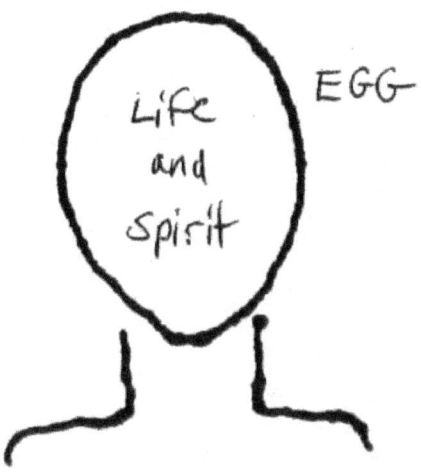

Your state of mind is very important and should be maintained throughout your life. Your answers should not be in the absolute but perceived in the non-absolute. I wish you well and that you have a fruitful life.

There are secrets of the master that one should consider as part of their vocation. You will need to practice the following aspects as it is pertinent to your discipline. I, myself, have been practicing it for 53 years.

1. You must perceive the drawing paper or canvas as a transparent surface. (Glass-like-material). This will enable you to perceive images in a given spatial presentation. It will also help you to see things three dimensionally. The sketch below will clarify for you the way to perceive.

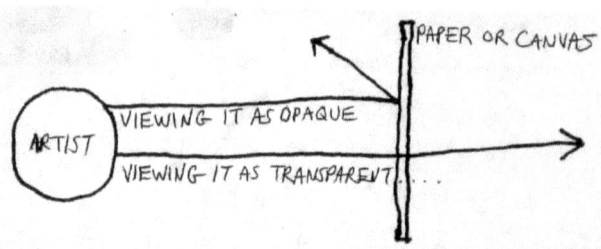

A quote by Matisse: "The outside world and the inside world, they are both transparent." This quote should give you the insight/sights to achieving great results in your world.

2. Zen: I find this exercise as very exciting in its form. I have practiced it extensively and eventually it became part and parcel to my abilities. You will notice by the diagram presented that the egg (raw) is placed between firth thumb and the finger. You will automatically take what must be at the fingertips to have life-like drawing or painting. (The egg should be placed on the inside.)

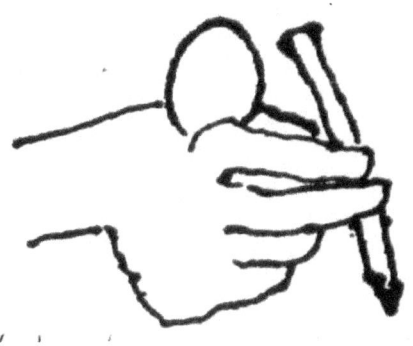

I broke at least 30 eggs before I got the hang of it.

There is a quote I'm taking out of a book *"Maestro Renoir you paint such beautiful females, how do you do it?"*

Renoir replies to the two women, "I paint with my penis." Renoir is implying that his brush is looked upon as an organ (penis) and his color/pigments are looked at as sperms, "life and spirit". This is a novel way of the previous statement to the students. Life and spirit are two issues for a great master. It is very important to be very serious about the comment he made to women. This is not a joking matter it is presented the realm of insight and revelation.

One could spend a lot of time in forming concepts pertaining to conditions. Art schools and universities and academies develop their programs around the concepts from conditions. Such philosophy leads one to develop their skills in the dynamics of absolutes. There is a tragedy that evolves from such programs as it hampers inspiration and self-esteem.

*"Moon in the Dewdrop,"* a book on Zen, translated by Kazuaki Tanahashi is an excellent source for inspiration that will lead you to nature. On page 90, paragraph 2, I quote the following "Conditions do not arouse it." The central source for the book is with this paragraph.

What are some of the examples of condition that I should be aware of?

1. Perceiving outlines is an absolute

2. Titles attached to a given form is an absolute

3. Having a system of approach is a condition.

4. To like something is external and therefore is a condition.

5. To love nature is to have infinity and the spirit.

6. Nature gives you clarity and freedom.

7. Nature is constantly being plastic and, therefore, is always in the state of an "<u>answer.</u>"

Things that have "answers" do not have conditions.

I know as a beginning student you will have man in the past, my students in the same puzzlement of thinking. You should read carefully what I have presented to you and not disagree with any of it, I am the voice of nature and roar like a lion.

What I have just presented will make your life fuller and exciting. The one who comes from nature is always a greater teacher.

You need to purchase a rat trap (large) for this presentation. This trap will remain as your teacher for the rest of your life. You will continuously learn from it and apply it to your composition. It is important to realize that this training-aid is the vehicle for understanding and comprehending nature.

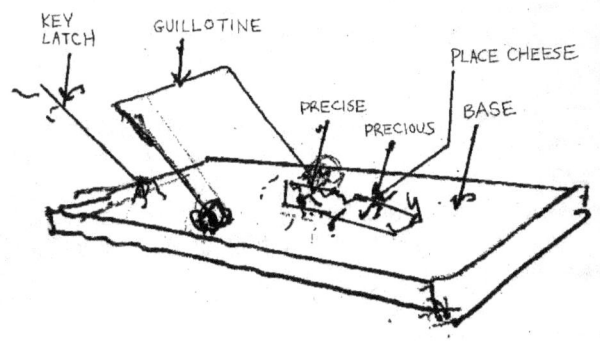

Notice in the diagram, above, the relationship of each component as found on the surface of the base. I want to assure you that I don't take this presentation lightly.

The purpose of the trap is to take away the life of the rat. Each of the components are designed and to be viewed as precious. When viewing the trap, one begins to realize the importance of the trap in relation to the fingers. A tremendous amount of sensitivity and caution is at the foremost part of the mind. You need to apply that same sensitivity when you are making a drawing or a sculpture piece. The placement of the key latch over the gadget must be precisely placed for it to work properly. The cheese is to attract the rat so that this gadget could work accurately. The cheese must be placed on that flat part, as shown in the diagram, prior to setting the trap. The entire procedure is like doing a drawing or sculpture piece.

I have considerable results from my studio, and it was evident that the student improved immensely.

The intensity of each component is in a transition constant state. The tension from the spring got into the base and in the guillotine component of the trap. One realizes that there is considerable pressing in holding down the guillotine so that the key latch can be placed over it and attaching it to the appendix found in the cheese location. One begins to realize that the tension in the guillotine continues to which is precise on the trap. This trap is telling you that nature is constant and monumental. I have found, myself, on many occasions doing a drawing to sculpture that has the same intensity as the trap.

I am 71 years old, and the trap is with me today. It is a wonderful teacher, and it is too bad that it is not a woman.

Many scholars tried to provide a simple answer to the meaning of design. In 1992-94 there were seminars devoted to various principles formation, about design, clarifies the principles and its character in art.

It is always best to define "design" for beginning students. There are so many interpretations of design that I found it confusing for the student to understand fully.

The rat trap gives you the intensity you should be viewed in the context of design.

It will help you to express yourself and at the same time increase your ability to perform artistically. The lion and the rat trap have the same intensity.

Nature is always cocked and is transitional within the framework of time and space.

*We need to clarify the use of a clock in this presentation. It is important that you understand that the clock was an example in portraying the functioning of nature. The clock is designed by human being and uses nature to fulfill its goals.

This presentation, plus those in the senses, must be viewed in the realm of insights and revolution. You must, also, consider these presentations not in a chronological order. It is important that you perceive their application as a profound element in their composition.

I am beginning with the High Renaissance period as a point of history of quest. There is so much information prior to the Renaissance at I would be involved in it for a great period of time.

This information will be beneficial to you in forming ideas and concepts to your composition. Let us begin with the following.

## Art and aesthetics: High Renaissance

1471-1519 AD

The Renaissance period had an enormous number of discoveries artistically an architecturally. It was a marvelous period for the young artist to apprentice under the great masters of the time,

Michelangelo's insight to nature changed and helped to develop the 20th century approach to aesthetics. I am presenting this quote from Michelangelo: "Dovrebbe vedere alle tutto nello un parte."

Translated to English- "<u>You must see the whole in the part</u>."

This philosophical thought is a tremendous insight in developing a total of a composition. There is a great sense of plasticity and freedom in the composition. You need to develop and record this insight as part and parcel to your vocabulary.

The second important development of the period was "chiaroscuro". The translation of it is light and dark. This element was to define and implement a sense of volume in the composition.

The third insight was mechanical in nature. It tended to destroy the spiritual part of a given composition. The reflection made to the definition of space as it recedes to a horizon line. The point perspective and the two-point perspective were perceived absolute. They were happy in resolving it mechanically –this aspects composition.

The fourth element that was implemented was a degree

of movement in the piece or pieces. This movement was portrayed as physical entity.

When it comes to color, of this period, one views the shape as the main emphasis and source for their composition.

It is best that you attain a book on the Renaissance as it will help you to view the paintings and sculptures properly.

**1561**: The late Renaissance is a period of great insights and revelation. I could only, this point in time, go in the direction of the academic artists of the period. Artists like Chiambiasco and Anniballi Carracci are both academicians that developed concepts leading to the absolutes. This period of information is still being used today among universities art department and academies. Formulas and systems slowly grew out of these thought processes. It eventually ended up as a rule-of-thumb. The artist from these schools of thought looked at themselves as having a certain type of trade. These artists are known today by the following title- Mannerists (in the manner of) Every time I view, the art from this period as stuffy and without content. I, personally, get constipated when seeing this period of art.

I had started earlier that one should not view this information chronologically. It is important to have it in your mind when we present the concepts in the $20^{th}$ century thought and principles. An artist must be a scholar to be tuned with nature. There are good things that were done and bad things that were done within each period. We need to begin, at this point and time, to develop our concepts so that we will eventually find ourselves in nature.

The lion took me to nature, and I realized how profoundly the history of quest is important to our creative thought.

What a wonderful book to have in your possession. The book is filled with non-dualistic concepts and ideas. You can learn a lot from this book as it opens a great vista of thinking. I have introduced this book to my graduates at Southern State University. There was a tremendous amount of excitement from my graduate students that they wanted to continue the subject into the next semester. Nondualism is the way to go in 21$^{st}$ century thinking. Let me, now; define the two words so that you may get a certain feeling and sensitivity.

**Western man**: Dualism-action expecting a rebuttal; or response oriental thinking, such as Zen.

**Non-dualism**: action without any response or reference. The person in this category is coming from the spirit. The composition grows organically out of the spirit.

All art, that which is great, will be the art of the future. It is this avenue of thinking that has led me into Zen and nature. I am therefore a Zen master.

Consider and examine thoroughly both aspects of aesthetics. The Notan book will give you the leverage to greatness.

*Notan: the dark and Light Principle of Design, Dorr Brothwell and Morlys Frey ©1968

Non-dualism will train you to practice its substance for the rest of your life. Nondualism's spirit is where the style germinates and reaches its fulfillment.

You must first come with greatness so that the pupil will have confidence in you.

I will now list the qualities that make a great person:

1. The string and nut will help establish in plasticity in those things that are plastic. (Practice it for 3 years)

2. The rat trap. The tension from the rat trap proves that form is transitional and reaches a precious and precise. You should practice this daily for 3 months)

3. The balloon gives us the dynamics that form must grow and leads us to Nondualism. The holding of the balloon, maintaining it, gives you the power of what composition ought to be in your artwork, ("the outline of the form escapes me" Cezanne us telling us that the artist should practice everything that is perceptional. You must see inside of yourself continuously for the rest of your life. It is a daily learning experience.) Practice for 3 years

4. Balance and structure: it is one of the hardest things to develop for a student. The easiest way to approach it is with the rat trap. The holding bar goes to that little notch helping to sustain life and preciousness. Life in itself is balance and structure. Practice the rest of your life.

You must understand that nature is your teacher.

Everything that I gave you comes out of nature and the spirit. You need to carefully read everything that I have presented to you. I want you to reach greatness, as I have with my assistants. That talking with them gives me the greatest joy and happiness. I am constantly learning from them even at my age.

Don't listen to someone who says they have a way of thinking. Don't listen to someone who 'likes" what they are doing. Don't listen to someone who says he is right, and they are wrong. You'll learn nothing from him. Don't listen to a person who has a great interest in technical approaches. Don't listen to a person who talks about size and measurement.

I have been confronted with many professors and artists who think in the above manner. They make me feel lonely and frustrated. I want to help them achieve greatness but have found myself spending energy foolishly. I hope these presentations that will be forthcoming will be fruitful to you, your dad, and to your students.

I am taking you to the mountaintop so that we will see great vistas. Let us start with the first step by practicing what I presented. I will wait for you at the mountaintop with open arms.

The Zen master always sits on the mountaintop. All his presentations are steps leading to the vistas of nature.

All my writings are steps to require practice. You cannot reach these goals unless you put it to use. I studied with two great artists, and I saw them at the mountaintop. They told me that it is a great struggle and will be part of your life.

A master always struggles to achieve beauty. He is the same as a tulip existing in the garden. The tulip loves being itself. It is there tuned in with its surroundings. That is monumental.

A tulip struggles and practices everyday its sensitivity. (Just like the rat trap)

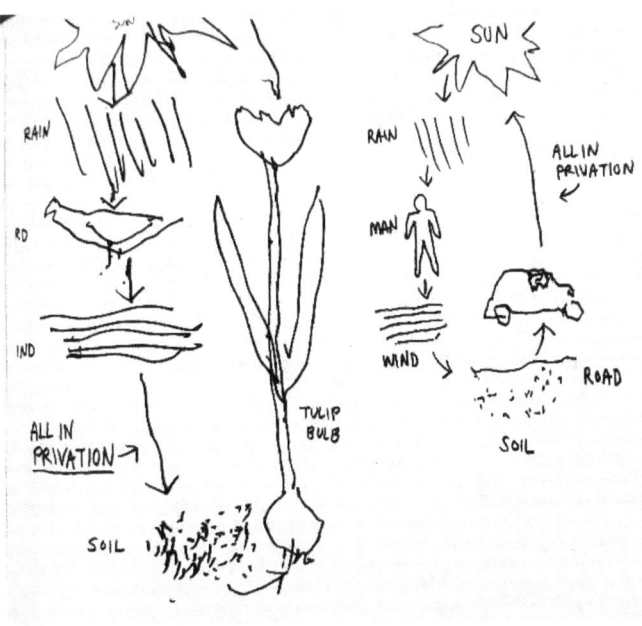

The two diagrams show us the importance of privation as part and parcel to beauty. We now realize that the intangible is always related to the tangible. Privation shoes us that beauty is monumental and represents the spirit of things. We should also consider that the intangible frees the immediate world. We should, also, consider privation as a vehicle to plasticity.

Within the realm of privation is the dynamics of design. We know that design must be plastic and that it leads us to monumental qualities. Design, therefore, must have an origin in the spirit and culminating to the whole of the composition.

As an artist and educator, you're on a difficult road in this chosen vocation. What I presented in the diagram must be experienced daily. Your studio is nature and nature is your spirit.

I'd like to quote Picasso: "I have trained myself to let nothing pass me by."

I have used his statement as part of my philosophy. Privation will always nourish you and it will inspire your thoughts. Love is always in privation. That is why it is beautiful.

**Nature is your teacher. –Michael Skop**

This book was transcribed from discussions and lectures over a period of days in 2003, when my father was 71 years old. The text and images were initially transcribed and scanned by a former Studio 70 student and artist, Alan Capasso. Ahna Skop executed the layout, cover, and edited the book.

Notes:

Notes:

Notes:

Notes:

Notes:

Notes:

Notes:

Notes:

Notes: